Frontispiece: *Distant views of the Olgas, dome-like rock features with foundations plunging thousands of metres into the earth.*

Pages 2-3: *Along the spectacular and winding Great Ocean Road, the Twelve Apostles are one of the most dramatic sights. These limestone stacks are slowly dissolving into the sea.*

Pages 4-5: *One of the most popular beaches on the Gold Coast, Coolangatta is on the New South Wales side—a mecca for surfers and family fun.*

Page 6: *Looking almost like a painting, the earthy colours of the Flinders Ranges change from soft pastels to vivid orange, as the sun makes its journey across the sky.*

Pages 8-9: *Nestling amongst the snow gums in a Victorian Alpine National Park is this old rustic, wooden gold fossicker's hut.*

Page 10: *The outback mailman uses a light plane to deliver the mail to his district, which could be scattered over thousands of square kilometres.*

Pages 12-13: *Even in this remote Tasmanian town of Sheffield, modernity has come to town in the shape of huge murals used to decorate historic old buildings.*

PHOTO CREDITS

Oliver Boch: front and back endpapers, 2-3, 6, 8-9, 10, 12-13, 14, 15, 22-23, 24-25, 34, 35 (bottom), 40, 41 (bottom), 47 (top left), 51 (centre), 55 (bottom), 58 (top right, centre and bottom), 60, 61 (bottom left), 63 (top and centre left), 65 (top left), 66 (top left and bottom), 70 (top right, centre and bottom right), 71, 73 (bottom), 74-75, 85 (bottom), 86-87, 93 (bottom), 95 (bottom), 97 (top left, centre and bottom right), 99 (top left and centre), 104, 105 (bottom), 107, 109 (bottom), 116 (top left and bottom), 118; **Photobank Singapore:** front cover, 16, 20, 21, 28, 36 (bottom), 45 (bottom), 46 (top), 56-57, 64 (bottom left), 68 (bottom), 78, 84, 93 (centre), 101 (centre left), 114 (bottom), 117 (top and bottom right), 119, Manfred Gottschalk; 26-27, 30-31 (top left), 42-43 (bottom), 61 (top, centre and bottom right), 64 (top), 109 (top right), Brian Lovell; 32, 42 (top left), 43 (top left), 58 (top left), 105 (top), Steve Vidler; 35 (top), 108, 120 (inset), David Messent; 37 (bottom), 41 (top), 43 (bottom right), Paul Steel; 44 (top), Luca Invernizzi Tettoni; 45 (top right), 52-53, 54, 55 (top), 59 (right), 63 (centre and bottom right), Wayne Lawler; 44 (bottom), 45 (centre), 66 (top right), 67, 70 (top left), 81 (inset), Rick Strange; 51 (top left), Sylvian Grandadam; 68 (top), 68-69 (centre), 79 (bottom), 117 (centre), 123 (bottom right), Dallas & John Heaton; 69 (top), 93 (top), 105 (centre), 120-121, 122 (bottom), 123 (bottom left), Pictor; 70 (bottom left), SG; 73 (top and centre), Didier Noirot; 79 (centre), Michael Gebicki; 90-91, 96 (top right), 109 (top left), Jean Kugler; 45 (top left), 51 (bottom), 63 (bottom left), 69 (bottom), 72, 80-81, 127, Photobank Singapore; **Topham Picturepoint:** 18, 67 (top right), 124; **Dave G. Houser:** 94, 95 (top left and right, centre); **Focus Team, Italy:** 33, 46 (bottom), 99 (top right), 115 (top left); **Chris Davis:** 55 (bottom), 60 (top left and right, bottom right), 66 (bottom left), 78, 86 (bottom right below), 112 (top left), 115 (bottom), 117 (bottom); 127 (bottom left); **Christine Osborne:** 47 (top right and bottom), 96 (bottom left and right), 97 (bottom left), 125 (bottom); **Richard I'Anson:** 4-5, 17, 48, 50, 62, 77, 85 (top), 101 (top right), 102, 115 (bottom); **Jill Gocher:** back cover, 38-39; **International Photobank:**1, 29, 30-31 (bottom), 36 (top), 37 (top), 49, 65 (top right, centre and bottom), 79 (top), 96 (top left), 101 (bottom left), 106, 112-113, 114 (top left and centre), 115 (top right); **Haga Library, Japan:** 82, 100, 101 (top left and bottom right); **HBL Network:** 43 (top right), 76, 92, 114 (top righjt), 122 (top left), 125 (centre), 126; **Bes Stock:** 59 (left), 83, 88-89, 109 (centre), 110-111; **Chris Davis:** 98, 99 (bottom left and right); **David Simson:** 97 (top right); **Bruce Postle, The Melbourne Moomba Festival:** 103 (top left and right); **Life File:** 103 (bottom left and right); **Camera Press Ltd:** 122 (top right), 123 (top right), 125 (top right); **The Advertiser, South Australia:** 123 (top left).

AUSTRALIA: THE LAND DOWN UNDER

© Times Editions Pte Ltd 1999
1 New Industrial Road
Singapore 536196
Email: te@corp.tpl.com.sg

Series Editor: K E Tan
Designer: Tuck Loong
Picture Researcher: Susan Jane A. Manuel
Production Manager: Anthoney Chua
Colour separation by United Graphic Pte Ltd, Singapore
Printed in Singapore

ISBN: 981 204 994 0

AUSTRALIA
THE LAND DOWN UNDER

AUSTRALIA
THE LAND DOWN UNDER

Text by
JILL GOCHER

TIMES EDITIONS

CONTENTS

INTRODUCTION

A ustralia is not known as the "Lucky Country" for nothing. This mineral-rich, ancient country is blessed with wide open spaces and fertile lands, surrounded by endless beaches and magnificent clear oceans. The land makes a perfect breeding ground for the friendly and easy-going people who inhabit its shores.

With a modern history dating back little more than 200 years—a short time span for the world's oldest continent—Australia easily compares with a younger version of America: a free country with a vibrant multicultural population in the throes of developing its personality and asserting a national identity.

The flavour of the country has changed radically from its colonial beginnings, when it was founded as a small British penal colony. With immigrants arriving from over one hundred and fifty countries and an increasingly urbanised population, the older Australian stereotype of a pioneer settler or outdoorsy adventurer has changed to a more sophisticated city dweller. The "true-blue Aussie" can be found only in the outback. Cultural mores of the "New Australians" have moulded the cultural, culinary and political climate of this intriguing land.

The country has blossomed to become an independent minded nation and an increasingly strong voice in world politics, especially concerning human rights issues and ecological salvation of the planet. When it was recently suggested that Australia's vast desert areas could become a perfect dumping ground for nuclear waste, the explosive "NO" that issued forth from all kinds of Australians had the idea dropped as hastily as it was suggested.

As their cause strengthens, Australia's original people, the Aborigines, are finding a louder voice for their proud heritage. Land and cultural rights are being supported with increasing vigour by many Australians and the Aborigines are no longer a forgotten people.

While money and business are no doubt as important to Australians as many other nationalities, the primary concern remains the quality of life and its enjoyment. "If it's no fun, then don't do it," could be adopted as an Aussie slogan and enjoyment of precious leisure time and personal friendships contribute to the country's laid-back atmosphere. Australia's great traditions of mateship and looking after your friends spring from the harsh early pioneer days.

Even though now the country is predominantly urbanised, Australians still like to think of themselves as robust outdoor types. Whether it is enjoying a beer and a barbecue in the summer sun, a day at the beach, or camping or fishing, being outdoors still appeals to most Aussies. Any holiday will see roads jammed with traffic as city dwellers head out of town, back to their rural roots.

But at the same time, Australia is by no means a nation of "drongoes" (or fools). The country is a world leader in branches of medical science, technological innovations, telecommunications, computer science, literary pursuits, and of course sports, whether it be football, golf, swimming and tennis or the Sydney Olympics in the year 2000.

These giant termite mounds (left) are one of the most distinctive geographical features of the Kimberley in Western Australia. Above: The pristine beauty of an untrammelled nature can be enjoyed at places like the superb Triplet Falls in Victoria's Otway State Forest.

HISTORY AND
THE AUSTRALIANS

Australia's modern history is so short that junior school children are well versed in its highlights almost as soon as they learn to read. While the indigenous Aboriginal people have existed in the continent for over 40,000 years, the brief but colourful modern European history reaches back just over 200 years to January 1788 when the First Fleet sailed into Botany Bay with the colony's first governor, Captain Arthur Phillip at the helm, ready to start a new colony.

Exploration and discovery play a major part in the story. While adventurous Asian fishermen and Arab traders had no doubt been visiting the barren northern coast for centuries, documented sightings made by Portuguese mariners and later, Dutch explorers, were recorded only after the 17th century.

The first well-documented European sighting was in 1606 by Dutchman Willem Jansz who sailed through Torres Strait. Spaniard Luis Vaez de Torres who sailed there the same year gave the Straits his name. Various Dutch sightings of the northwestern coast, included Dirk Hartog in 1618 and Frederik de Houtman in 1619, but there was little to arouse interest in possession.

Having already colonised Indonesia, the Dutch had little need for this barren addition to their empire and after naming it New Holland, left it well alone. Eventually the mercantile Dutch East India Company (VOC), encouraged further survey of the southern continent, and in 1642-3 Abel Tasman reached the island of Tasmania.

Discoveries continued for more than a century as the Dutch mapped the coast from Tasmania, west across the Great Australian Bight and north along the western entirety, miraculously missing the fertile eastern shores. The honour for that discovery goes to the British mariner, Capt. James Cook, who reached those hospitable shores more than 160 years later on 19 April 1770.

Britain at this time was in the beginning throes of her "industrial revolution". A huge increase in crime occurred as people flocked to the cities searching for work and money in newly established factories. Hunger and deprivation forced people to steal food to keep alive, and men were jailed for stealing a loaf of bread. Stealing a sheep was a hanging offence or sometimes, life imprisonment, with the result that prisons and later, the prison hulks anchored in the Thames, were filled to bursting with petty criminals.

Prisoners were shipped off as cheap labour to the new world colonies of America but after the American Revolution in 1783, it was necessary to find a new locale to send the convicts. In 1783, Cook's botanist, Sir Joseph Banks, suggested Botany Bay as a suitable site and without further ado, plans were made to establish a new colony on Botany Bay on the continent of New South Wales.

Australia's new Parliament House in Canberra (left) leaves many visitors gasping in astonishment. The stark modernity of the building contrasts strongly with the more gracious lines of its former structure. Above: Australians respect valour, and each year, all over the country, people flock to pay their respects to the "Old Diggers" as they march down the main city streets.

After dismissing Botany Bay as unsuitable, the First Fleet settled on a new site at Port Jackson, slightly to the north on what is now Sydney Harbour, described as "the finest natural harbour in the world". The Fleet comprised 11 ships with a complement of 730 convicts, both male and female, four companies of marines, and enough food and livestock to last for two years. Two years later in 1790, the Second Fleet arrived with supplies and more convicts, and a third fleet in 1791.

The beginnings were not auspicious. Brutal guards, an inhospitable foreign climate, and poor conditions took their toll. The colony teetered off to a slow start and a long struggle for survival. The young colony was completely dependent on supplies imported from Britain and the already established Norfolk Island settlement for 16 years until farms could be established.

Development continued more or less as expected with fights, corruption amongst the officers, and general squabbles that were par for the course for a new colony. Governors changed, conditions worsened, then emancipation of prisoners was introduced so that freed prisoners were given citizen's rights and lands. With free labour and free land, many of the officers found means to earn a much higher income than that supplied by Her Majesty's government and for many, riches were quickly and easily acquired.

One of the most far-reaching aspects of Australia's early history was the discovery by an officer named John Macarthur that sheep fared well in the southern grazing lands. He began breeding high quality merino sheep and their wool was to become one of Australia's most important exports for more than a century. As the old saying goes, "Australia rode to wealth on the sheep's back."

The 30s and 40s saw new colonies opened in Western Australia, Tasmania and Victoria's Port Phillip Bay, giving opportunities for free settlers to establish properties. Transportation of prisoners was abolished in 1852 to the eastern colonies and in 1868 to the west after over 168,000 convicts had been transported.

It was the discovery of gold that really put Australia on the map. The early 1850s saw gold discovered in several sites. Honour for the first big discovery goes to a Californian miner named Edward Hargraves. In April 1851 he made a strike near Bathurst, outside Sydney. Particularly large finds in Ballarat, Bendigo and Castlemaine followed, centring gold exploration in Victoria. Easy to mine and easy to find, it provided the road to riches for men from all walks of life, with Australia exporting more than £124 million of gold in the first ten years.

Fearing trouble, the authorities tried to quell news of these early discoveries, but there was no stopping the excitement. Rumours were rife and people arrived on the goldfields in droves. Sailors deserted their ships, farmers their farms, whole towns were emptied of men as gold fever struck. Chinese immigrants came in their thousands as did Irish and Englishmen, Americans and Europeans,

The raising of the British flag in 1788 at Sydney Cove in the new colony of New South Wales. The first group of settlers was brought from England under the command of Captain Arthur Phillip.

flooding the fields with hopeful workers. In ten years, Victoria's population exploded five-fold from less than 100,000 to over half a million—part of the boom that was to last until the late 19th century.

The government edict that all gold discovered belonged to the state was quickly ignored and the rule was abandoned. Mining licences were issued instead and for the price of thirty shillings (three dollars), anyone could become a gold prospector. The diligence of the Chinese and their success as both miners and market gardeners led to race riots and an aversion to hardworking Asian labour that was to colour Australian immigration laws for another century.

Not all miners were successful and many diversified to become farmers, traders, shopkeepers and settlers. Others turned to the more profitable, if dangerous occupation of bushranger—and tales of the daring exploits of famous bushrangers like Ned Kelly pepper Australian folklore.

For the first twenty or so years, the people of the new colony were content to stay close to the settlement. Struggling for survival there was little inclination to explore outer areas. People were still unaware of the country's size, and speculation that it was two separate islands persisted. Then, due to an ever increasing need for farmland and grazing areas for the burgeoning sheep industry, the Blue Mountains were successfully tackled in 1813. Explorers Blaxland, Lawson and Wentworth found a way through the previously impassable mountains, to rich grazing lands beyond. The then governor, Macquarie, ordered a road to open the land for new settlement.

Many of Australia's early exploration attempts however, such as the Burke and Wills expedition of 1860 to cross the continent from south to north, ended in disaster. The harsh climate and a people unaccustomed to the country's tough conditions, caused many mistakes which could probably have been avoided with a little know-how and assistance from Aboriginal guides. The brave struggles of these early explorers epitomised the spirit of the new colony as men fought against all odds to document the new land. By the 1860s most of Australia had been explored.

Until the late 19th century when the call to federate became increasingly strong, small colonies existed independently. Federation finally arrived on 1 January 1901 as the first meeting of parliament was held in Melbourne, the beginning of a never-ending rivalry between Sydney and Melbourne. Six states were formed—New South Wales, Victoria, Queensland, South Australia, Western Australia, and Tasmania. The Australian Federal Territory which contains the capital city of Canberra and the Northern Territory were created later.

While the newly formed Commonwealth Government was awarded very strict guidelines with specific powers, most of the powers were left to the states. The states were given equal representation in the Federal Government regardless of size or population—an anomaly that exists until today.

Although Australia became a fully fledged nation, her loyalty to the mother country of Britain was never questioned. During both World War I and II, Australia sent troops to defend Britain. These troops fought with great courage to defend their mother country. Heroic tales of Australian bravery abound. Particular battles such as Gallipoli, Tobruk, and the Kokoda Trail in New Guinea, where the soldiers fought fiercely against almost overwhelming odds in appalling conditions, are remembered with reverence until today. On 25 April each year, ANZAC (Australian and New Zealand Army Corps) Day celebrates the heroism of Australian soldiers. Parades of returned soldiers, both young and old are held in capital cities, and a minute's silence observed in respect for those brave lives lost in past battles.

It was the USA, not Britain, that was to protect Australia in the latter days of World War II. Britain's reserves of men and supplies were seriously depleted, with little left to offer. All her remaining energies went to defending Europe rather than the far-flung colonies of Australia, Malaya and Singapore.

Post-war Australia saw much needed development of the country with the help of an increased population. Between 1947 and 1968, many "New Australians" were enticed with a £10 assisted passage from England and a dozen European countries. In the past fifty years, over five million immigrants from over 150 countries have made Australia their home. These "New Australians" helped to build the country that exists today.

PART ONE
AN ANCIENT LAND

An idle glance at a map of Australia can do little to reveal the lonely grandeur of this singular continent. It will fail to show the endless miles of dazzling surf beaches and craggy headlands that announce the almost 37,000 km of coastline—or the clear incandescent quality of the southern light that seems to shimmer with purity as it illuminates the land. It will miss the colours of Australia—the stark beauty of the red desert, the browns, ochres and golds of antiquated rock formations at sunset and the purplish blues of distant mountains, a supernatural palette of soft and earthy hues.

The map will reveal, however the size of this, the world's largest island, or smallest continent. Its 7.6 million sq km is comparable to continental USA, or to the whole of Europe, excluding Russia. It will reveal an almost mountainless terrain and vast areas of desert lowlands, eroded by the harsh elements for longer than time itself. Scratchy map markings along the northeastern seaboard translate into the world's longest coral reef. Australia's Great Barrier Reef stretches for over 2,000 km, a long-time barrier to the huge swells of the Pacific Ocean.

In a rapidly urbanising world, Australian ideals hold fast to the power of nature and an untrammelled wilderness—free from the encroachments of man. Even now with only 18 million people populating its almost limitless hectares, there are more than a few murmurs of "enough, enough".

The world's flattest and driest continent, Australia is also the oldest. It was over 160 million years ago that the great southern landmass of Gondwanaland split—a continental drift of epic proportions as Antarctica, South America, Africa and India drifted apart, away from Australia and the remnants of Gondwana.

This ancient land has rested, undisturbed by turbulence, by volcanoes or earthquakes for over 100 million years. Situated at the centre of a vast tectonic plate, it is the most stable landmass in the world. One only has to spend a night in the desert to feel this stillness and the humming silence that has reigned for millennia. Its even more antiquated geological history, however, dates back over three or more billion years, and astonishingly, signs of these ancient times are still in evidence in some of the remote wilderness areas, preserved for posterity in 12 UN World Heritage Sites.

As this aged land eroded away, rich mineral deposits were bared while mountainous regions were reduced to little more than hills. Mt Kosciusko, the highest peak of the once mighty Great Dividing Range, rises to a mere 2,228 m (7,310 feet).

Away from the fertile coastal plains, arid Central Australia consists of wide swathes of flat, almost featureless red desert, broken with rocky outcrops like the immense Ayers Rock (Uluru) and the Olgas (Kata Tjuta), that stand as silent sentinels of earlier times.

To many people, the Australian landscape is harsh, without the soft greens of Europe and much of Asia. D. H. Lawrence called it "an invisible beauty." It takes time for the eye to adjust to these harsher colours, the grander vistas, a more vibrant, rawer version of nature. It takes time for this invisible beauty to touch the soul.

The rugged point of the giant termite mound (left) provides an interesting contrast to the rounded trunk of the Boab tree in Western Australia's Kimberley. Above: Remote Kings Canyon in the Northern Territory is a landscape of ancient eroded rocky valleys where once raging rivers ran.

THE GREAT OUTBACK

Beyond the cities and the fertile coastal plains of the east lies the majority of the country, the outback or rural Australia. Here is another world, far away from the urban sophistication of the cities. The outback encompasses endless miles of the semi-arid grazing lands that have helped to build Australia's wealth—where one cattle station can encompass more area than a small European state. Small towns dot the outback, some consisting of no more than a pub and possibly, a post office.

Much of Australia's outback is desert or semi-desert—vast wide landscapes of barren, red earthed land that reach to a distant horizon. Punctuated by craggy rock outcrops and the silent majesty of the occasional gum tree, these rugged landscapes exist nowhere else in the world. Yet as harsh as it is, there is a stark grandeur about these endless stretches of red earth that sweep beyond human vision. Sweeping stretches of bright reddish orange earth are enlivened with the odd scattering of stunted dark-green mulga and spindly spinifax scrub.

The Living Desert

At first glance the desert appears lifeless. Yet it teems with life—an endless array of wild creatures that have adapted to the harsh climates. Many of its inhabitants are nocturnal, burrowing into the ground to escape the hot sun, only to emerge in the cool of the evening, a fine time to hunt for food. Reptiles, lizards, small rodents and insects populate the desert in their thousands.

The Red Centre—Ayer's Rock

Formed from an ancient mountainous land mass millions of years ago, Ayers Rock (called "Uluru" by the ancient Aborigines), is the world's largest rock monolith. The Aborigines considered it a sacred place and for millennia it has been the focus of Aboriginal cultural and territorial interaction. No amount of photographs can ever truly prepare a visitor for a face-to-face encounter. Pictures simply cannot convey the immensity, the silent power that it exudes, in spite of the millions of tourists' footsteps that have trod there.

The colour is never constant. From hour to hour it changes hue, reflecting the passing of the sun across its varied surfaces. From deep morning gold it changes to hazy blues and deep purples as the sun heads towards its zenith, before dropping westwards and illuminating the vast rock in glowing golds and deep, deep orange reds.

At 9.4 km in circumference, and over 350 m high, Uluru was handed back to its original owners, the Anangu people along, with the nearby monolithic Olgas (Kata Tjuta) in October 1985. The owners then leased it back to the federal government and now they manage it in conjunction with Parks Australia. Acting on advice of the Anangu people they will preserve and protect these sacred sites for generations to come.

THE GREAT DIVIDING RANGE

The continental divide known as the Great Dividing Range runs all the way from Cape York in the far north to the western border of Victoria and extending down into Tasmania. Eroded millennia ago, these rugged mountains are not high, but they form a major landmark on the Australian landscape, dividing the fertile eastern seaboard from the drier Western Plains.

Part of the Great Dividing Range are the hazy Blue Mountains just outside Sydney—one of the more popular wild beauty spots in the country—a wonderland of impassable rocky escarpments and magnificent views to a distant sea. Dramatic rushing waterfalls and smaller cascades fall over rugged plunging cliffs, to vast valleys below. Trekking trails lead through eucalyptus forests and outside the major tourist spots, the forests are almost people-free. Once the Blue Mountains were the home of ancient Aboriginal tribes whose sacred sites are dotted among the caves and crannies of the forest.

Further south are the Snowy Mountains, home to Australia's highest mountain, Mt Kosciusko. The highest mountain reigns over the state's largest protected reserve, the Kosciusko National Park, that covers an area of 6,900 sq km. The winter months see boundless snow that turns the mountains into a white wonderland and centre of a thriving ski business. Several resorts cater to skiers from around the country.

Australia specialises in wilderness areas and an hour or two west of Sydney are the Blue Mountains (left), one of the most visited areas in Australia. The rock formation known as Three Sisters is one of the Blue Mountains' best known landmarks. Top: Victoria's Grampians are characterised by huge hanging rocks, known as "balconies". Above: Contrary to popular perception, Australia is not all desert, as the Apsley Falls of Oxley Wild Rivers National Park dramatically illustrate.

The Snowy Mountains Scheme

Also within the Snowy Mountains is the brilliantly conceived Snowy Mountains Hydroelectric Scheme, an $800 million project that lasted from 1949 to 1974.

With Australia's low rainfalls, water conservation has always been of prime importance and schemes to maximise water use have long been proposed. The first major project, the Snowy Mountains Scheme, was designed with the two-fold purpose of diverting water to arid western agricultural areas like the Riverina and to provide cheap hydroelectricity, while boosting post-World War II development. The brilliant scheme encompasses a complex of sixteen extensive dams, a series of pipes and 161 km (100 miles) of tunnels to divert the water, passing it through massive generators in the seven power stations creating cheap hydroelectric power. In times of water shortage, water is released from the dams, while in times of plenty, it is diverted to the storage dams, ensuring a constant supply of the life-sustaining liquid.

Apart from changing the face of Australian agriculture (and the Snowy Mountains), the scheme provided much needed employment for thousands of workers, many of them refugees from war-torn Europe. The scheme was praised for its bold concepts, one of the largest such schemes in the world. While it is the biggest in Australia, the Snowy Mountains Scheme is one of several such projects that have been developed in the east.

*F*aces of the mountain. Left: Although the the Snowy Mountains enjoy only a short winter season, the few months of snow attract an enthusiastic crowd of skiers at the alpine resorts. Perisher Valley is one of the most popular. Right: One of the power stations of the massive Snowy Mountains Scheme that generates electricity by harnessing the enormous power of water rushing downstream. Below: The Alps in the summer take on a different hue as this view of Mt Kosciusko shows.

AUSTRALIA'S MAJESTIC RIVERS

For such a large country Australia's rivers are few. The world's driest continent outside the Antarctic is not bestowed with numerous water courses of any dimension. The flow of the Murray-Darling River system, Australia's largest, is a drop in the ocean compared to the great rivers of the Mississippi, or the Ganges that streams from the mountain vastness of the Himalayas. One year of flow of the Murray equals just nine days of its American counterpart, the Mississippi, or seven days of the Ganges, while of the mighty Amazon, a year's flow is equivalent to a startling one and a half days' flow.

Statistically speaking, the water flows are small, but ingenuity combined with creative thinking and high technology have managed to maximise the use of these rivers to create highly effective irrigation areas and hydroelectric power of affordable rates. While large areas of the Red Centre remain dry and arid, water has brought other areas a standard of agricultural viability that has them producing magnificent vineyards, and excellent wines, fruit, vegetables and all kinds of high quality produce in such abundance that there is plenty to export to many parts of the world.

The Murray

Australia's longest river, the Murray, meanders for over 2,500 km, gaining strength and volume as it is joined by the Darling and Lachlan rivers and their many tributaries on the long course to where it empties into the sea, south of Adelaide. This river is the main water source for much of the eastern Australian plains, and irrigation areas established along the banks have become some of Australia's main food producing regions. Cattle and sheep, fruits, rice, grapes, wheat, maize and sorghum are all grown very successfully under irrigation systems.

In earlier times huge paddle-steamers would ply up and down the river carrying diggers to the goldfields, and serving the needs of early pastoralists as well as transporting cargo to points east. Although the passenger business died out with the advent of railways in the early 1900s, steamers carried cargoes until the 1950s. Today the steamers are used mostly for the recreation of tourists.

Views of the river. Above: Once these paddle-steamers were the main form of transport on the rivers. Today they transport sightseeing tourist as they relax. Right: Even more relaxed is this fisherman, sitting, waiting for a bite on the Murray River.

THE EASTERN SEABOARD

From southeastern Victoria to the tip of the Cape York Peninsula, the mighty Pacific Ocean borders the east coast. While the Great Barrier Reef protects the northern reaches of the coast from the ocean swells, the rest of the coastline is a run of golden sand beaches and long sweeps of surf, rolling in undisturbed across the Pacific Ocean.

Australia's beaches are the best in the world. From southeastern Victoria to the rugged southern coast of New South Wales, the fishing towns of Eden and Merimbula, Bateman's Bay and Ulladulla, form a focus to the verdant hinterland. Mile after mile of magnificent beaches line the shores to as far as Kiama and Wollongong, then to Sydney's splendid harbours and littorals. North of Sydney are the beautiful Nambucca Heads and Coff's Harbour, then to the most easterly beaches of Byron Bay and Brunswick Heads. Further north again is the Gold Coast and Surfer's Paradise, the Sunshine Coast, Maroochydore and Fraser Island—these endless beach names rolls easily off the tongue, as easily as the cold clear waves roll to the shores.

Fishermen standing close to Australia's most easterly point, on one of the rocky shorelines of Byron Bay (left). Once a major whaling station, Byron Bay today is a popular centre of alternative lifestylers. Above: Sydney, located on the magnificent Sydney Harbour, is regarded as one of the most beautifully situated cities in the world. Right: Long littorals of white coral sand and aquamarine waters characterise the Whitsunday Islands, just south of the Great Barrier Reef.

A LAND OF PLENTY

I n contrast to many of Australia's near neighbours, the country enjoys the happy position of a vast and almost inexhaustible supply of land, while labour is quite expensive—there are no peasant farmers in the country but rather farmers and titled landholders.

During the first half of the 20th century, Australia's primary industry was so successful to the point that it brought the country a wealth that was to sustain early development. Wool production was already an established industry, when the gold discoveries of the 1850s caused another burst of wealth for the young colonies.

Since the early days of the colony, sheep played an important part in Australia's economy. Top: Wily sheep dogs are used to round up recalcitrant merinos. Above: Sheep on the hoof—these woolly animals are expected to walk themselves to new grazing fields. Top right: Shearing sheds are a source of interest of out-of-towners. The fastest recorded time for shearing a sheep is less than a minute. Right: Wealth on the hoof. These beef cattle in the Northern Territory are being rounded up ready for transportation to southern markets.

Following spread: Ride'em cowboy. The annual Alice Springs Rodeo provides thrills and spills for the participants and plenty of action and beer for the spectators.

Acres of Sheep and Countless Cattle

Beef and wool are Australia's most important primary exports—a long-time source of wealth. Wool was Australia's first major export, started early in the new settlement when gentleman-farmer, ex-Rum Corps officer, John MacArthur, began breeding experiments with Spanish merino sheep. He quickly saw the potential of this as an export crop for the new colony and spent the rest of his life improving the breed.

The beginnings of the British industrial revolution meant that spinning and weaving mills were setting up across Britain causing an almost insatiable demand for fine wool. The Australian farmers were kept busy. By the 1850s the sheep population had soared to 60 million and by the early 20th century, Australia supplied some 70 per cent of the London wool market, with over 100 million sheep.

In the '80s Australia produced 60 per cent of the world's wool but growing competition from synthetics and development of new markets have caused a decline. Today, while wool remains a major foreign exchange earner many sheep farmers are experimenting with exotic animals like llamas, cashmere goat and angora goat's mohair.

Australia is also one of the world's largest exporters of beef and veal to over 100 countries. Vast cattle stations in outback Queensland and New South Wales, with water supplied from artesian bores raise more than 30 breeds of cattle, including the hump-backed Brahmins and the red-and-white Herefords. Grass-fed and generally unadulterated with hormones and synthetic feeds, Australian beef is one of the best in the world.

The dairy side of the beef business, too, is a booming business with over a billion dollars worth of produce exported each year. From the sublime cheeses of King Island to the milk and cheese products of Bega, the quality is as good as the tastes produced.

Rollicking Rodeos

Just like the American Wild West, the Australian outback has its own rugged cowboys, although they are generally known as stockmen. When it comes down to it, stockmen or cowboys, they can ride a bucking bull, and sit just as well on a horse and wear a tall cowboy hat. When the rodeo comes to town, it is time for a rollicking good time for all. Besides the travelling cowboys, who follow the rodeos professionally in the hope of winning the handsome purses offered, local boys come in on the scene too.

Strategically placed loudspeakers broadcast tinny strains of sentimental country music, as beer gets downed in large quantities. Stockmen and cowboys prepare themselves for the events, tying on leather chaps to protect their legs and binding their hands with strong gloves, before facing the wild steers. Rodeos, whether at Alice Springs or any of the other outback towns present a fabulous scene—a living adventure straight out of a movie and a slice of "the real Australia".

Wonder Wheat
—Australia's Rice Fields

The vast wheat fields of Australia make it one of the country's largest industries and Australia is the world's fourth largest wheat grower of high quality, high protein wheats.

Today wheat farmers are diversifying to a wider variety of grains as European-style breads and pastas have created a niche market. Barley, sorghum, mung beans, oats, canola, chick peas, and other grains that will be consumed both at home and abroad are being introduced.

Wheat fields sprawl for kilometres along the Great Plains of South Australia (below). Right, top: The combine harvester revolutionised wheat harvesting when it was introduced several decades ago. Right, bottom: Wheat leftovers are neatly packaged into hay bales to be used for animal feed.

Mineral Riches—A Modern Gold Rush

Australia's primary source of wealth started with the 1850s gold rush—a forerunner of great things to come. In this mineral-rich country, mining has brought unsurpassed wealth to the country. The ancient, eroded dry land has revealed rich concentrations of minerals close to the earth's surface, making both discovery and mining an uncomplicated matter.

Indeed when Lang Hancock flew over the vast Pilbarra iron ore deposits in the 1950s, he noticed the mountains glistening with an almost pure quality of ore. Today the 1.5 billion dollar BHP Pilbarra iron ore plant pumps out an astonishing 2 to 2.5 million tonnes of processed hot briquetted iron, ready for shipping to steel mills around the world.

Minerals form the country's largest and richest export. More coal is exported from here than any other country and this mineral alone accounts for some 12 per cent of the country's total exports. The coal supplies of Australia alone are enough to support the whole world's requirements for several centuries—astonishing statistics! Iron ore too is a major export, as are gold, coke, bauxite, alumina and aluminium, petroleum and gas. Diamonds and precious gems are found too, especially the unique opals that exist barely anywhere else in the world and certainly not in the same quantities! Titanium, uranium, base metals and other rare metals are all important exports.

A wealth of opals. Above: The world in an opal—here some magnificent opal chips are displayed fresh from the mine. Left: Raw opals for sale in Colin Williams opal shop at Coober Pedy, Australia's opal centre. Below: Opals are dug from deep tunnels under the ground in the Coober Pedy area. It is fortunate as the searing heat would make life unbearable, if mines were above ground.

*O*ther wealth—Australia's mineral wealth takes many forms. Far top left: Tourists watch a gold panning demonstration at Sovereign Hill, one of Victoria's first gold-mining areas. Left: The massive open-cut iron ore mine at Tom Price in the Hamersley Range of Western Australia demonstrates the huge extent of the countries' mineral deposits.

DARWIN—AUSTRALIA'S LAST FRONTIER

Probably Australia's most evocative and colourful capital, Darwin is very much a frontier town, a town on the edge of change. This relaxed and cosmopolitan melting pot is Australia's closest link to Asia—a crossroads where Asia and Europe meet on Australian soil. While modern new buildings and hotels are changing its face, Darwin retains the atmosphere of a frontier town, aided in part by a large transient population.

Darwin's importance lies in its proximity to the myriad attractions of the "Top End". It is the gateway to adventure territory—and from here people can set off to explore the remote national parks like Kakadu and Arnhem Land, Katherine Gorge, mangrove forests and their abundant bird life, and ancient caves decorated long ago by the Aborigines.

It is also the beginning (or the end) of The Track, the long straight road that runs south to Katherine and then to Alice Springs, right through the red heart of the country. Anyone who follows it far enough, will end up in the southern capital of Adelaide, some 3,000 km to the south.

Visions of the outback. The dramatic geological formations of Stanley Chasm (far top left) and the fresh waters of the Ormiston Gorge (far left) are just two faces of Australia's outback. Giant termite mounds (left) are a source of fascination to tourists as are the Aboriginal cave paintings (top right) of Kakadu National Park. This Aboriginal burial mound (top left) is a version of the mounds found throughout the Northern Territory. Above: Alice Springs in the centre of Australia is a long ride down "The Track" from Darwin.

OUTLYING AUSTRALIA —ISLAND POSSESSIONS

Australia's little known island possessions are scattered way beyond her shores. Small and generally economically unimportant, the islands are little capsules of quirky history.

Pine-shrouded Norfolk Island has a short but colourful history. After starting out as a penal colony for the irredeemable, a "place for the extremest punishment short of death", it was later relinquished and handed over to the descendants of the famous HMS Bounty mutiny—who were unhappy with the ship's tyrannical captain, William Bligh. Located 1,600 km from the Australian coast, it is now a popular tourist destination.

Closer to the coast (500 km) is Lord Howe Island, a subtropical paradise. Its untouched forests and fine beaches have caused its inclusion in the World Heritage List. Christmas Island to the northwest started life as a phosphate colony with Malay and Chinese workers brought from Singapore. The extraordinary primal vegetation, the annual red crab migration and varied bird life, incredible diving and a high-rolling casino, set it apart —a colonial oddity as is the relatively nearby Cocos (Keeling) Islands, a coralline atoll populated largely by coconut plantations. Even less well known are the remote Coral Sea Islands, stretching over one million sq km between New Caledonia and the Great Barrier Reef. Proclaimed as the Coral Seas Islands Territory in 1969 these uninhabited islands form two vast national marine nature parks—a treasure house of untouched marine species.

Way down south in the icy waters of the Southern Ocean, some 2,500 nautical miles from Fremantle are the Australian sub-antarctic possessions, Heard and McDonald Islands. These gale-swept islands have few permanent settlements outside large colonies of seals and other marine bird life. To the other side of Australia in the southeast, Macquarie Island has a permanent research station of scientists who man the Macquarie Island Nature Reserve, richly populated with seals, albatross, and the world's largest colony of King Penguins.

Lonely places. Australia's outlying possessions are even less populated than the mainland. Some islands, like this Great Barrier Reef island (above) are not populated at all, while Kangaroo Island (below) is becoming a secondary tourist destination. Norfolk Island (far top right and bottom) has a long history and is no longer a convict colony but rather a quiet holiday destination. Port Arthur (far top left), once a tough convict settlement, now attracts visitors to see its well-preserved colonial architecture.

PART TWO
FLORA AND FAUNA

Cut off from the rest of the world for over 100 million years, Australia is a treasure house of unique flora and fauna. The geographic isolation allowed the development of an extraordinary wildlife, unlike that of any other country. While Africa and India have big game animals, and Asia has elephants, tigers, monkeys and orang-utan, Australia is a cornucopia of singular animals which have uniquely adapted to the harsh environment. Many are quite small but not the red kangaroo that grows to over two metres tall, or the vicious saltwater crocodiles that can reach over 10 metres.

Here is a collection of contradictory creatures: birds that don't fly, egg-laying marsupials, bear-like koalas that are really marsupials and kangaroos that box. While most people have heard of Australia's better known animal inhabitants like the kangaroo, wallaby, koala, platypus and possibly the wombat, who has heard of the quokkas (rat-like kangaroo from Western Australia), the numbats and bilbies (or bandicoots) that are lurking in the bush? The list is endless and surprising.

The wild dog, known as the dingo, still inhabits the grassy plains of the interior while wallabies are a smaller grey version of their cousin the kangaroo. The big, cuddly wombat eats roots and leaves, and together with the echidnas, goannas, wallaroos and Tasmanian devils, form part of the varied world of strange creatures.

Bird life too is diverse. Forests echo with the raucous cackle of the laughing kookaburra—a kind of mocking laugh that has beguiled beleaguered explorers of the past. No one who has ever witnessed the spectacular mating dance of the lyrebird as he exhibits his finery to a prospective mate, will go away without being enthralled. The bush is alive with brilliant colours, such as that of the blood-red rosellas and flocks of white, sulphur-crested cockatoos, who always have a guard on duty while they feed. Noisy pink and grey galahs, known for their stupidity, are easily seen on the Western Plains. Budgerigars, better known as caged pets around the world are a native of Australia, living in huge flocks of a thousand or more. Feeding off flowery nectar, the rainbow lorikeets are a living palette of primary colours. Shaggy emus, a cousin of the African ostrich, roam in the outback far away from man and his predatory ways.

Even spiders loom large in local lore and Australians, with their irreverent ways, have made songs and even named a beer after the redback, a poisonous spider commonly found in woodpiles. Snakes, many of them poisonous, lizards, goannas, and crocodiles of the fresh- and saltwater varieties offer potential hazards to intrepid explorers.

While it is the animal kingdom that grabs the attention, the flora too is varied and unique. Australia's most well-known tree is the eucalypt, better known as the gum tree with over 500 species dotting the country. Mulgas and brushwood dot the outback, while highlands support alpine vegetation. Far to the west, springtime is heralded with wildflowers carpeting broad swathes of the Western state in a colourful magnificence. Perhaps Australia's best loved native plant is the wattle tree. Its golden flowers exude a sweet scent that perfumes the bush with a distinct fragrance that is typically Australian.

Unique flora and fauna is an Australian specialty as these grass trees in Queensland's Noosa National Park (left) and the red kangaroo (above), inhabitant of the Australian outback, illustrate.

THE LIVING FORESTS

Once, some 120 million years ago, the whole of continental Australia was covered with lush, living forest. As the country began to dry up about the time Gondwanaland drifted apart, the forest cover retreated, to less than 1 per cent of the total land area.

Disdained and unappreciated by early settlers, who preferred the trees of their green home country, large tracts of forest were cleared to make way for farmlands. The forests became grazing land for herds of dairy cattle and endless acres of wheatlands. The settlers planted their homesteads with the more familiar European species like willows, poplars, ash, elms and oaks. City parks still feature predominantly European species.

Recognition of the importance of the forests has grown over the past few decades. These unique natural habitats are home to a wide variety of species which include more than one fifth of the country's bird species and one quarter of the reptiles. Today forest covers some 0.3 per cent of the land and large tracts can be still found scattered along eastern Australia from Tasmania to Cape York. Pride in Australia's unique wilderness areas is growing stronger and strict laws have been implemented to preserve them for future generations.

More through good fortune than great planning, some of the world's oldest tropical rainforests survive almost intact in far North Queensland, which is designated a World Heritage area. From Cooktown, high up on Cape Tribulation down to Mossman, the thick covering of rainforest remains. Dating back some 100 million years, it has survived not only the incredible changes that were wrought on the earth's surface, but more recently, the efforts of loggers and governments to convert trees to cash. Now, with the efforts of the "Greenies" (ecologically minded folk) and possibly, the growing lure of the tourist dollar, the forests are here to stay.

Lush greens of the rainforest come in a variety of hues, from that of the palm (above) to those of the mountain ash and fern tree of Victoria's Dandenong Ranges National Park (right). The rainforest of the Cape Tribulation area (left) encompasses a full spectrum of hues while the mist-swathed temperate beech forest (below) is otherworldy in its beauty.

Overleaf: Rock formations in the Kakadu Wilderness. Rock ferns sprout forth from the crevices in this stratified sandstone crevices in the cliff face. The fronds catch moisture and humus from the crevices during the monsoonal wet season.

Preserving Australia's Natural Heritage

Recognition of Australia's capricious wilderness areas has earned Australia a place on the World Heritage Register. In fact over the past 14 years, 12 sites in Australia have been recognised by the UNESCO World Heritage Convention. While the sites are all nature oriented rather than urban, many meet the criteria for both cultural and natural heritage preservation. Sites are scattered across the Australian mainland, Lord Howe Island and Tasmania. The Great Barrier Reef is an obvious contender as is the Tasmanian wilderness area of the Franklin River. Covering 20 per cent of the island, it is one of only three temperate wilderness areas remaining in the southern hemisphere. Shark Bay on the western coast is an important reserve—a home to many species of endangered animals, while Kakadu in the Northern territory has gained international prominence as a tourist destination, no doubt assisted by the movie *Crocodile Dundee.*

While recognition of the richness of its natural heritage came relatively late in its 200 year history, Australian people now are amongst the most environmentally sensitive in the world. Much of Australia's wilderness is protected by national parks and state reserves where offenders are treated with severity.

The trend to protect the environment has become a major national cause. In an attempt to undo the earlier damage, landowners are replanting the land cleared by their forefathers with new seedlings and trees. Environmental awards are flying thick and fast. The ecologically viable Olympic Village at Sydney's Homebush, where a previously denuded area has been restored, has already received an award.

A heritage worth preserving. The bark renewing properties of this smooth barked Apple Gum (left) contrasts interestingly with normal trees which renew their leaves. In Queensland's tropical north, this mangrove tree (top), is propped up by a silt root system that not only keeps it aloft in the soft substrates, but also helps the plant to absorb oxygen. Above: Bungle Bungle Mountains in the Purnululu National Park of Western Australia is an extraordinary example of weathering, where the striated rocks have been worn smooth and round by eons of sun and rain activity.

NATIONAL PARKS

Five per cent of the country's total land area is designated as national park, with over 500 reserves or national parks spread across the country. In fact the world's oldest monument to nature, the Royal National Park, can be found within Australia's boundaries. Gazetted around 1879, it is located just south of Sydney.

The Australian conservation authorities feel that within national parkland, things should be left in their natural state, without signs of the hand of man. In an almost sacred trust to keep for future generations, there are strict prohibitions on mining, logging, on commercial enterprise of any kind. Nothing but nature at its most pristine is allowed.

Australia's national parks do not encompass only forests. Many parks consist of ancient rock formations like these of the Devil's Marbles (above) in the Northern Territory, or the inimitable Bungle Bungle (preceding pages and right) in Western Australia. Even more dramatic are these rock formations of Oxley's Lookout (below) in Karijini National Park, or this Meteorite Crater in Wolfe's Creek (bottom), Western Australia.

Kakadu National Park

About 250 km east of Darwin is Kakadu, one of Australia's great wilderness areas and a UN World Heritage site. Bordered in the east by the great Arnhem Land escarpment, the park boundaries stretch for 200 km south and cover an area of 6,144 sq km.

Within the park are Aboriginal sites that have been inhabited continuously for 25,000 years—no mere dead relic but a living heritage that contain some of the richest concentrations of rock art in the world. The descendants of these ancient cave dwellers now own the park and as well as acting as guides to the increasing numbers of tourists, lease the site back to the government who allows sensitive low impact tourism. The flood plains of Kakadu's wetland ecosystem support a vibrant migratory birdlife—and dangerous saltwater crocodiles (*crocodylus porposus*) that can grow to over 7 m in length.

The sights of Kakadu National Park in the Northern Territory range from the monsoonal lowland forest where giant termite mounds can be found (above) to the rugged Obiri Rock (left), the site of millennia old Aboriginal rock art.

Tasmania's Great Wilderness

Apart from having the world's cleanest air and water in the inhabited world, Tasmania, Australia's largest island, has the best preserved, temperate rainforests and the highest proportion of national parks (25 per cent).

Tasmania's wilderness areas have not been preserved without a fight. The Pedder River area was lost to a massive hydroelectric project and dam and a similar fate awaited the wilderness areas around Tasmania's Franklin River. It was saved by the actions of thousands of protesters who joined forces to bring attention to the plight of this untouched area. After a lot of media attention, and arrests of some 1,500 protesters, many who chained themselves to the trucks and tractors of the loggers and dam developers, the Federal government stepped in and declared the area to be safe.

New regulations were introduced to ensure the preservation of the wilderness and the Franklin-Gordon Wild Rivers region has been internationally recognised as a UN World Heritage area, kept for the enjoyment and use of future generations.

The river has become popular as a rafting expedition, the best way to see this wild area, much of which is impenetrable forest. Expensive and extensive expeditions have been arranged by tour companies for those wanting to explore.

Taken from the top is this Alpine inclined view of Hobart (left) while the sublime Russell Falls are a picture of pristine beauty (top). A purple sea of lavender flowers (centre) awaits visitors to northeast Tasmania. Lake St Clair National Park (above left) and Cradle Mountain (above right) are more of the multifaceted faces of Tasmania's wild places.

AUSTRALIA'S UNIQUE SPECIES

As Australia drifted off from the other continents, it changed the history of the species. Cut off from the more advanced predators of other continents, these primitive life forms continued to survive undisturbed in Australia, developing new strains of the species.

Most intriguing of Australia's weirdly diverse species are the mammals of which the marsupials and monotremes are the most bizarre examples. Of the two species of monotremes, the best known is the platypus—an evolutionary muck-up beyond belief. With the bill of a duck, the tail of a beaver, webbed feet and fur of an otter, it lays reptilian eggs and suckles its young like a mammal. The spiny anteater or echidna is its similarly incongruous cousin.

The marsupials are no less incongruous. Kangaroos and koalas, possums, wombats and wallabies are some of the better known examples. Their distinguishing characteristic is the birth of half-developed young which are then brought to maturity in a nippled pouch where they live until old enough to move about unaided.

The little known native flora, too, of the Australian bush is unique and diverse. Besides the inimitable gum tree, the myriad blooms are unparalleled in any other country. Banksia, waratah, kangaroo paw, Christmas bells and native rose, Sturt's Desert Pea, boronia and bottlebrush, grevillea and spider flowers abound.

Of all the wildflower areas, the southwest region of Western Australia enjoys the richest abundance. It is in the spring that colourful flowers carpet broad swathes of the normally arid countryside with bright colours.

Wild and not all beautiful, Australia's species are one of a kind. This freshwater crocodile (left) is one of Australia's fiercer species unlike the cute wallaby in the long grasses (above). The brush-tailed possum (right) and the platypus (below) are not at all ferocious, unlike the Tasmanian devil (bottom left). The sand goanna (below right) is only dangerous to the bird eggs it likes to steal from the nest.

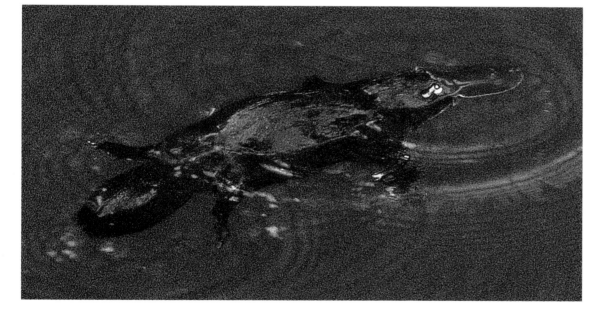

*W*attle trees (top left) scent the air while providing splashes of vivid gold to a sometimes barren landscape. Bottom left: Looking just like the inspiration for a Ken Done design, this rocky Northern Territory land has sprouted numerous wildflowers and shrubs after the rain. Above top left: The Golden Banksia adds an incandescent glow to its surroundings while Western Australia's Sturt's Desert Pea (above top right) is easily recognisable. Above centre left: The Waratah, the state flower of New South Wales, has a dense globular head of red flowers surrounded by red bracts. Above centre right: This pink bottlebrush can be seen around Sydney town while the desert eucalyptus (above) exists far out in the Pinnacles of Western Australia's Nambung National Park.

Eucalypts—The Australian Gum Tree

From the starkly beautiful snow gums with their eerie ash grey trunks to the towering mountain ash—the tallest flowering plant in the world—the myriad strains of eucalyptus tree have an austere kind of beauty.

Over 550 species of eucalypts, better known as gum trees, make Australia the gum tree capital of the world. While some species can be found outside the country, in New Guinea, Indonesia and even as far as Vietnam, the vast majority are singularly Australian, scattered across the country in forests, plantations or standing singly, a lone white trunked specimen adding emphasis to a rocky gully.

The hard timber of the Tasmanian blue gum is used for railway sleepers while others are harvested for their superb fine grains. The leaves of all eucalypt species contain a fragrant oil which embodies healing medicinal properties. The sight of a stately gum tree is an acquired taste and once acquired becomes a popular favourite. The koalas in fact will eat nothing else.

Eucalypts are almost exclusively Australian—providing sustenance to native animals like this cuddly koala (right) who seems to be sleeping after a particularly heavy lunch. Ghost Gums are one of the more majestic styles of eucalypt varieties as these three pictures (above) will reveal.

The Cuddly Koala

Cutest of all the Australian animals is the cuddly koala. Often misnamed as a bear it is in fact a marsupial. Like the kangaroo, the koala too, keeps its young in a pouch until they are able to move around, after which they cling to the mother's back.

Found mostly in the east, kolas love to feast on the leaves of certain species of eucalypts, their sole source of food. They live in the trees and rarely come to the ground, spending their lives up high. These adorable creatures are favourites of visitors to the country and "to cuddle a koala" is a special treat for anyone.

The Kangaroo

Highlighted in this showcase of isolated evolution is the distinctive kangaroo. Found on the Australian coat of arms, it is the country's most recognisable symbol. More than 50 species of kangaroo bound their way across the country, each one keeping their young, known as joeys, in their pouch.

These prolific breeders can expand their numbers very quickly when conditions are right, so much so that in many areas they are regarded by farmers as a pest and over three million are culled annually.

The kangaroo varies from the giant big reds that grow to more than 2 m high and can leap up to 9 m in a single bound, to smaller species as big as rats and the tiny tree climbers that can't hop at all. Similar in appearance, the wallaby is a cousin to the kangaroo, differing in colour and stature.

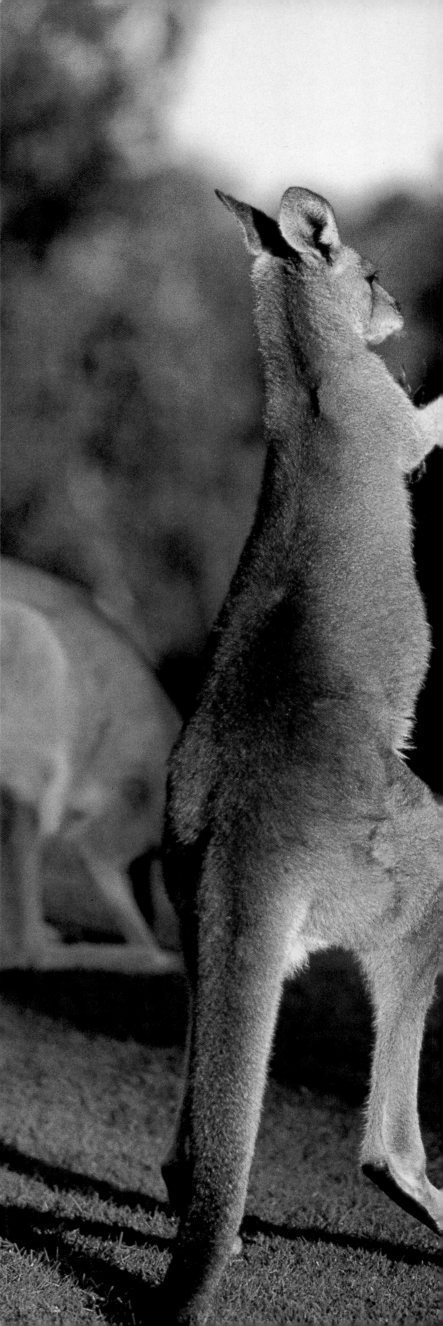

Signs, signs everywhere—one of Australia's more evocative signs (top) warning of impending kangaroos and wombats. Above: This orphaned kangaroo joey will no doubt be fed by eye-dropper and milk until it is old enough to fend for itself.

*K*ung-fu fighting it is not, but kangaroos (left) love to box, especially the big reds. This little quokka (below) is a long-time descendant of the creatures that fooled the Dutch. Thinking they were large rats, the Dutch named Rottnest (Ratnest) Island after them, when they first landed there a century or more ago.

What's in a Name

Someone must have had a great sense of humour when naming Australian animal species. Numbat (*Myrmecobius fasciatus*) is an Aboriginal name given to a small 500-gramme endangered marsupial—a pointy nosed red-and-white striped creature who lives on termites. Quokka, also an aboriginal name, is a short-tailed wallaby found primarily in the west on Rottnest Island. The name "rottnest" (rat nest) was given by a Dutch mariner who thought that the quokkas were very large rats.

The Rabbit

Knowing little about ecological matters, the early settlers brought rabbits to Australia which they planned to breed for hunting, with little idea of how well the Australian climate would suit them. In England, rabbits were little more than a cute addition to the country landscape. In Australia, they multiplied at a horrendous rate eating the native vegetation and causing starvation amongst many indigenous species. As the population rose to an estimated 500 million, almost reaching plague proportions, something needed to be done and a disease was introduced. Fatal only to rabbits, it soon brought the numbers down to manageable proportions.

BIRDS—COLOURS IN THE WILDERNESS

Australia has 745 birds species and 400 endemic species. They represent a broad spectrum, from the tiny honeyeaters that flit from flower to flower to the giant emu, the second largest bird in the world. Wedge-tailed eagles too are one of the largest of their species. While the sulphur-crested cockatoo is known around the world for its ability to talk, in its natural environment its call is a discordant shriek.

It is quite possible that Australia's bird species are more colourful and evocative than elsewhere. The Australian grey bush is enlivened by a turquoise flash of a kingfisher. The sparse Victorian forest is alive with the ringing call of a bellbird, known to be one of nature's best mimics.

Seagulls and myriad wading birds inhabit Australia's sweeping coastline and northern wetlands. Living by the coast are the delightful pelicans whose beak, according to legend "can hold more than its belly can". Constructed of flexible skin, it stretches to infinite limits when the fishing is good.

Birds galore. An abundance of birds can be found within the confines of this vast continent such as these pink and grey galahs (right), Northern Territory parrot (top left), and cassowary (top right), whose sharp claws can gouge a fatal blow. Above: A new taste—today the Australian emu quite often ends up on the plate. Far left: The mocking sounds of the laughing kookaburra can frequently be heard ringing through the Australian bush. Left: "What a wonderful bird is the pelican, its beak can hold more than its belly can." The clumsy but lovable pelican is one of Australia's favourite and most visible birds. As it catches more fish, its beak stretches to accommodate the extra load.

BENEATH THE SEAS

The clean cold oceans that surround this giant island are teeming with marine life. Here in the colder southern waters lurk the predatory killer great white sharks—the species that "Jaws" was modelled after. And these are not the only species. There are hammerheads, moray eels, giant potato cods and reef sharks. Fish species are numerous and some of the world's best-eating fish come from these southern waters. Who can deny the exquisite taste of fresh whiting and flathead, or the silver bream—a fish fit for a king.

The Great Barrier Reef

The Great Barrier Reef, stretching over 2,000 km along the northeast coast of Australia, is the world's most extensive coral reef. It was formed after the last Ice Age when rising waters drowned parts of the coastal plains. Many of the islands on the Reef are drowned mountains, although some, such as Lizard Island and Dunk Island are true coral cays, built over the millennia by hard shelled coral creatures known as polyps who live and die there, slowly building up a reef.

The deeper waters of the reef are home to over 350 varieties of hard corals and countless more soft varieties—a wonderland of species. The hard mushroom, staghorn and brain corals, contrast dramatically with the brilliant colours of the softer strains. Giant clams, up to one metre across, moray eels, giant cods, green and hawksbill turtles, stingrays, cowries, fans, gorgonians and corals are all protected and part of the Great Barrier Reef Marine Park, one of Australia's 12 World Heritage Sites.

While most sharks are not dangerous, their reputation precedes them. The Great White Shark (left) is one of the more dangerous varieties. This hard coral (above) is just one of the hundreds of varieties to be found on Australia's Great Barrier Reef as is this pink coral trout (right). Below: Hardy's reef, part of the Great Barrier Reef that stretches for over 2,000 kilometres along the north Australian coastline.

The Playful Porpoises of Shark Bay

Located at the centre of Western Australia's long coastline is the broad and shallow Shark Bay, home to large families of dolphins. With a lively intelligence, these lovable grey creatures have beguiled humans for centuries with their playfulness and willingness to make friends.

In the midst of Shark Bay, the World Heritage area known as Monkey Mia is drawing visitors from around the world. Visitors have the chance of a dolphin encounter as the dolphins swim close to shore for their human encounter.

The visitors stand waist-deep in water to feed and fondle the dolphins. The latter's strong powers of communication have allowed this strange encounter, where the dolphins know they are safe from predators. Started several years ago, when fishermen cleaning their fish threw scraps into the sea, word got around amongst the dolphin community and they were soon appearing, waiting to be hand-fed.

PART THREE

PEOPLE AND CUSTOMS

What a cultural potpourri of people it is that makes up the Australian population. Whether blonde or brunette, fair skin or tan, Australia today has many faces. Immigrants from over 150 countries have brought their traditions and customs to their new homeland enriching Australia's heritage, and broadening the cultural base as it becomes a truly multicultural society.

This "sunburnt country" image of rugged outdoorsy types living in the bush is a far cry from the reality. Australia is of one of the world's most urbanised societies—a multicultural mix of city dwellers where over 80 per cent of the population live in eight large cities. Less than 15 per cent live on the land and only some 6 per cent of the people work as farmers or other land related jobs.

Multicultural Australia is still a relatively new phenomenon that has evolved since the end of World War II and taken on new strengths in the past twenty years. While early immigration stemmed solely from Britain, it expanded in the 1950s to include northern and eastern Europe. Inevitably, with more enlightened thinking, Australia's geographical position was recognised and Australia opened the doors to its near northern neighbours. Now, the country boasts a sizeable Vietnamese and Cambodian population as well growing numbers from other Asian countries. The defunct "White Australia Policy" has given way to the "Tolerance and respect for all races" policy—a vast improvement that meets with approval from the majority.

Australia's oldest inhabitants, the Aborigines, have given "separate lives" a new meaning. Until recently, there has been little positive interaction between the Aborigines and the rest of the Australian population, if at all. But the same more enlightened attitude has led to a growing recognition of the rights and needs of these peoples and their place in the community.

Australia's unique form of popular culture is easy to parody but not easy to ignore. Much of Australiana centres around food icons. It is a land of Cherry Ripes and Violet Crumble Bars, of Jaffas and Minties, of steaming hot "Four and Twenty" meat pies smothered in tomato sauce at a winter football match. The most recognisable icon of all is Vegemite. This thick black coloured yeast extract is smeared on hot buttered toast and eaten with great enthusiasm from the time kids learn how to eat.

Australians have developed their own slang, a colourful patois that derives from the Cockney slang of those early British settlers. From the "g'daye mate" that is recognised around the world, to the easy-going "no worries" kind of attitude, Australians embrace a casual lifestyle filled with as few problems as possible.

Egalitarian Australia is a land where everyone is equal, whether rich or poor, Christian, Buddhist or agnostic. While Australia is nominally Christian, it is a society of religious freedom. The early British settlers brought Christianity to the shores, followed later with every religion under the sun. Today, religions are as diverse as the ethnic backgrounds of the people. Christians of many denominations co-exist happily with those of Jewish or Orthodox derivations. Sikhs and Hindus are as well accepted as are the growing numbers of Buddhists. Afghan camel herders brought Islam some time late last century and today mosques can be found spread across the country, catering to yet another wave of newcomers.

The face of Australia is as varied as these two faces of an old style explorer (left) and this pretty young city-dweller surrounded by flowers (above). Today the face of Australia encompasses old and young, men and women, from over 150 countries.

AN ANCIENT PEOPLE

Dating back over 40,000 years, Australia's Aboriginal society has the longest continuous cultural history on earth. Once the Aborigines lived across the continent, a nomadic people who wandered in small tribal groups, living in harmony with each other and their environment. The tribes spoke many different languages, developed different cultures and traditions, all the time keeping strong spiritual connections to the land that supported them.

Although they had no written language, education of the young was by word of mouth, passed down from generation to generation, the lore of the land, and the laws of nature. Self-expression came through dynamic and evocative painting, using natural materials of ochres, clays, charcoal and lime paste, to decorate their bodies, the interiors of caves, rocks and the bark of certain trees.

After decades of misunderstandings and injustices with the newer Australians, programs of "assimilation" and misguided assistance, the Aborigines are regaining an identity, salvaging racial pride and ethnic origins. Attempts at assimilation programs have been largely dropped and in appreciation of the cultural richness and spiritual depth, native title issues are giving access to the traditional lands.

Body decoration (top and right) still plays an important part in the lives of traditional Aborigines, especially when they are taking part in ceremonial events. Others choose to ignore tradition, opting for easy-to-wear Western gear (left and above).

Overleaf: Whether it's body art, drawings on a rock or a canvas, Aboriginal art is instantly recognisable with its distinctive patterns and imagery. White dots are used to outline the main figures which themselves are composed of dots.
Inset: Body painting uses a lot of white to depict animal shapes and to produce the broad stripes across the face as well as the typical hand patterns on the body.

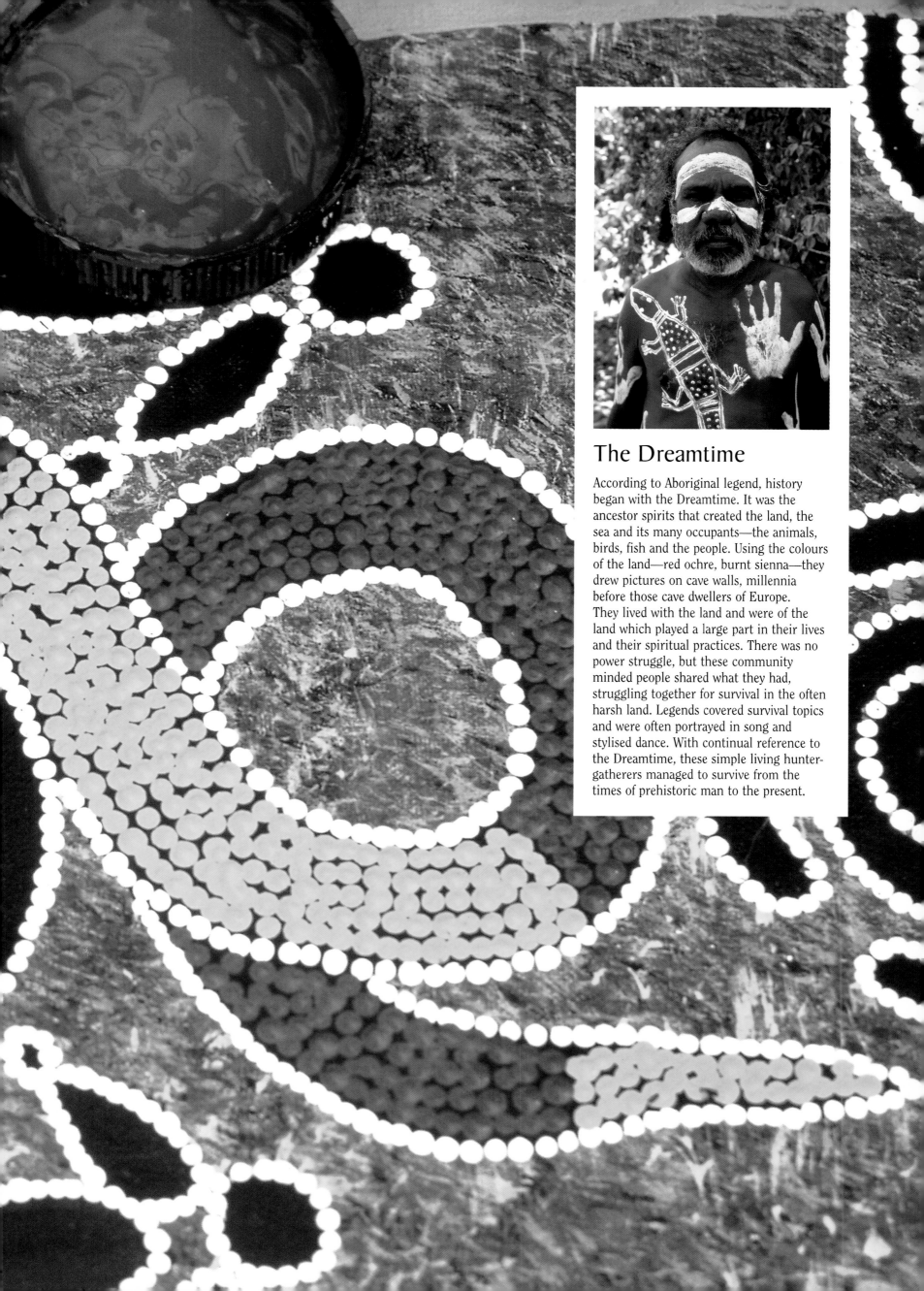

The Dreamtime

According to Aboriginal legend, history began with the Dreamtime. It was the ancestor spirits that created the land, the sea and its many occupants—the animals, birds, fish and the people. Using the colours of the land—red ochre, burnt sienna—they drew pictures on cave walls, millennia before those cave dwellers of Europe. They lived with the land and were of the land which played a large part in their lives and their spiritual practices. There was no power struggle, but these community minded people shared what they had, struggling together for survival in the often harsh land. Legends covered survival topics and were often portrayed in song and stylised dance. With continual reference to the Dreamtime, these simple living hunter-gatherers managed to survive from the times of prehistoric man to the present.

Corroborees

Ritual gatherings known as *corroborees* are a celebration of dancing, singing, and storytelling, one of the best known of the aboriginal get-togethers. Music is provided by a number of primitive but evocative sounding instruments like the *didgeridoo*, which when heard for the first time can raise hairs on the arms, so powerful and evocative are the notes that emanate from this hollow wooden tube. A haunting, humming kind of sound, it is said to echo the humming of the silent desert. The music is enhanced with clap sticks and sometimes boomerangs or clubs beaten together as instruments of rhythm.

Body painting plays an important part in tribal ceremonies. Distinctive markings are made with white lime paste, feather down, blood and ochre—each line has a different meaning.

This corroborees *re-enactment (above) gives outsiders an idea of the dynamism of Aboriginal traditional dance. Top: Clapping sticks provide the rhythm for any music or dance situation. Right: The* didgeridoo *is probably the most evocative sounding of all the instruments used in* corroborees. *Magnificent body painting is sometimes utilised in traditional ceremonies like this* didgeridoo *player (far right).*

AUSTRALIANA—AUSTRALIA'S POPULAR CULTURE

When Aussie actor Paul Hogan launched his popular advertising campaign in America exhorting folks to "put another shrimp on the barbie" it was quite an accurate portrayal of the Australian ethos. The "barbie" is still a strong focal point of Australian culture.

Trendy restaurants and glossy magazines portray a sophisticated audience, yet it is the beer and barbecue mentality that still lies at the heart of most Australians. While barbecues may now include marinated steaks and shish kebabs rather than sausages and chops, and guests may drink a good wine rather than beer, the desire to stand out in the open and have some drinks with the mates is as strong as ever. If there is a football game or a cricket match to drink along with, so much the better.

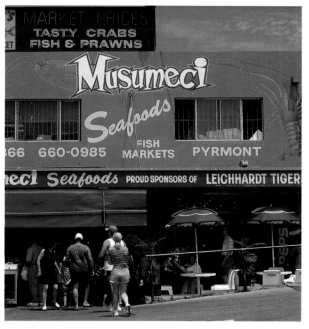

Australiana—A Language

Australia's unique language can often mystify newcomers and foreigners. Many words are derived from Aboriginal beginnings, others from Cockney and others, well, have just evolved. While "G'day" is known by almost all, how many non-Australians are familiar with a "chook" (chicken) or a "bludger" (a lazy person).

As a term of endearment, or familiarity, Christian names are shortened and everything has an "o" or "ie" tacked to the end of it. A "journo" is a journalist, "compo" is worker's compensation, a "garbo" is a garbage collector, and a "yobbo" is often a bit of a "lair", an uncouth person, while a "postie" delivers letters, and everyone likes a "barbie" or "barbecue".

Australians value their leisure time and come weekends everyone heads to the hills, or at least out of doors. Whether it is picnicking in the bush (left), buying up a load of seafood (above) or enjoying a barbecue (top), the most important aspect is taking it easy, even if it means downing a drink or two at the Birdsville Pub (overleaf).

At the Gold Coast

Tourist mecca of Australia, the epitome of touristic good times—sun, sea and sand, boozing, gambling and a vivid nightlife—is the Gold Coast, a 35-kilometre strip of surf beaches that stretches from Tweed Heads in northern New South Wales, through Coolangatta, Kirra, Currumbin and Palm Beach to the hub, the centre of it all—Surfer's Paradise.

The Gold Coast is or tries to be all things to all people. The myriad attractions include casinos, shops, restaurants and theme parks, koalas to hug and rosellas to feed, while the number one drawing card is the magnificent surf beaches and hot sunny weather.

Australia's People of the Sea

With splendid surfing beaches scattered around much of the country, it is no surprise that surfing is one of Australia's national pastimes. Young boys take to the beach early learning how to read and ride the waves, and for many, it becomes a full-time occupation, with some even turning professional.

Surfing started early this century in 1902 when eccentric Sydney newspaper proprietor and editor W. H. Gocher took a daytime dip at a time when it was prohibited. He opened the doors to surfing after advertising his intention of taking a midday plunge in the waves, defying the restriction on daylight bathing.

Nothing happened. No heavy hand of the law descended on his shoulders. He continued his defiance of the law and the law continued to ignore. Quite soon, others followed his example and the neighbours began to worry about the value of real estate sinking—so disturbed were they by the "indecent" bathers in their neck-to-knee costumes.

By 1906 Bondi beach had a surf bathers' association—and others soon followed suit. Surfing had caught on. The first surfboards were brought in from Hawaii but they were long and cumbersome, suitable for Hawaii's giant waves. Lighter boards, first introduced in 1915, have continued to become lighter and more manoeuvrable. Australia has dominated the surfing scene for several decades.

*R*ide, ride, ride the wild surf. The surf and the sea play a big part in Aussie culture. Whether it's working together with a surf life-saving team like these men (far left), catching a perfect wave (top right), or preparing to row out to sea for training (above), the sea is the thing. Left: Enjoying a more placid seaside experience at the Brighton beach huts in Melbourne.

Preceding pages: Looking for all the world like a beach house, even the community centre of Byron Bay features seaside motifs on its huge wall murals.

A Day at the Races—Melbourne Cup

"The Cup" or the "Melbourne Cup" is Australia's premier race—a time when Australia stops stock still for the hallowed few minutes while the race is on. Everyone has a flutter (bet) on the race, whether it be grandmothers or children. Classrooms hold sweeps (sweepstakes), workers bet, the race is on and an almost unnatural silence envelops the country. In Melbourne, people are given an official public holiday while the rest of Australia looks on. Held at Flemington every year since 1861, it is the country's most prestigious race and a prime social event. Whether hobnobbing in the member's compound with champagne and caviar or out in the stalls with the hoi polloi, it is a social occasion and a time for enjoyment.

For jockeys, owners and trainers, it is the chance to make their name, as the winner carries a lot of prestige. In egalitarian Australia the "sport of kings" has become the sport of the people, and everyone enjoys the race whether at the course or listening to the radio or television. Of course, on and off course betting is an integral part of the day.

Excitement and colour abound at the annual Melbourne Cup. Whether it is parading a winning hat (top left and right), parading a wininng horse (left), hoping for a winner while betting on the Totalisator Agency Board (right) or actually watching a race (above), there is activity and a controlled excitement for all at the Cup.

THE NEW AUSTRALIANS

Today Australia is no more a "little England" but a broad multicultural country composed of people from many nations. Europeans and Asians have joined the growing numbers of New Australians and multiculturalism is Australia's new catch cry.

The new arrivals have changed the character of both the lives and palates of the country. As any traveller knows, one of the first ways to discover a new culture is through the cuisine and it is the country's cuisine that has changed most. Cappuccinos and espresso coffee are

as accepted as a milk-shake once was and every town has at least one Chinese restaurant. A newly arrived Greek woman considers fried rice as an Australian dish (it is Chinese or at least of Asian derivation).

The corner milk bar now sells Chinese sausage, European cheeses and pita bread along with the white sliced bread, blue boxed processed cheese and milk of earlier times. Those purveyors of Australiana, the local fish and chips shop and hamburger stores now sell salad and foccacios along with the traditional fare—an unheard of phenomenon just twenty years ago.

Australia is home to a vibrant mix of people such as this Lebanese Australian florist (above), Japanese Australian office workers (right), this imported dive instructor on Green Island (top left), or two young cuties on a Sydney shore (top right).

Food Streets and Ethnic Enclaves

Inner city areas abound with exciting new cuisines from a dozen countries. The explosion of tastes started in the small ethnic enclaves of the new immigrants that offer a smorgasbord of cheap and authentic traditional cuisines—Vietnamese, Lebanese, authentic Greek and Italian and other more exotic fares.

As new tastes become accepted, there is a spillover effect on mainstream cuisine and now there are so many fusion influences between diverse areas. Chefs are adventurous—putting together combinations of taste and texture that would previously have been unthinkable. Restaurants offer new combinations each week.

East meets West but also Vietnamese meets Italian, Cambodian meets Japanese. It is not a named style, such as Californian Cuisine, but with everybody having access to Australia's wonderful fresh ingredients and quality produce, the confluence of tastes is exciting and tantalising as Australia's own food styles evolve.

Multiculturalism means multifood as well, as illustrated by this Greek ice-cream seller in Sydney (left) or this Asian vegetable stall (centre) in Hobart, Tasmania. Top left: Paddy's Market in Sydney offers not only a wide range of handicrafts and knick-knacks but a smorgasbord of foods that include Tandoori chicken and Himalayan cuisine. Anything is possible. Above: St Kilda's Fitzroy Street may not be quite as sophisticated as Ackland Street, but Leo's Spaghetti Bar continues to dole out servings of pasta to new generations of Australians. Top right: A Sydney suburb offers Chinese smorgasbord right next to the chemist.

Australian Wine

Australian wines have risen to great heights in both quality and flavour in the past few years to the point where they are recognised internationally with some of the world's best.

Wine technology brought from Europe helped establish Australian wines early on. German vintners arriving late last century

settled in the new colony of South Australian and noting the ideal wine-growing land and climate of the Barossa Valley was similar to that of "the old country" founded vast wine estates. Today the sprawling Barossa Valley community produces some of the country's best wine and celebrates many German festivals. Needless to say, it has also become a major tourist attraction for both the excellent wines and wine tastings and the German community.

While some 60 per cent of all wines come from South Australia, other newer wine producing areas have been established to include New South Wales' Hunter Valley, Victoria's Great Western and Mildura regions, Western Australia's Swan Valley and the Margaret river. Small boutique wineries have sprung up as well as the large established wine growing areas. Victoria's Yarra Valley now includes some of the most accessible and productive of the country's wineries, offering cellar-door tastings, picnic provision and restaurant facilities. For a wine buff, Australia is a paradise.

Wine-making can be fun as demonstrated by these two foot-stomping, shoulder-clasping grape pressers (far left) at a Barossa Valley Wine Festival. Held every second year, it gives visitors a chance to sample the product (left) and German growers a chance to entertain with some traditional Bavarian music (above). Centre: The hills are alive ... with grapes in the Barossa Valley while a man checks the grape crop (top right) which will eventually end up as wine in barrels like these (top left).

FESTIVALS—AUSTRALIA CELEBRATES

Festivals in Australia are a time of celebration, rituals that usually involve quite a lot of beer drinking, or for some, wine and champagne. Whether it be a religious festival like Christmas or Easter, a feast of culture or music, a sporting event or straight-out good time affair, you can be sure that any festival will be a time for revelry and a fun-filled occasion.

But many of the festivals do enjoy a serious content. Film festivals showcasing new film offerings and the arts festivals showcasing arts, theatre, dance and drama from around the world are not to be missed occasions. Arts Festivals are held in most states while the Adelaide Festival of the Arts, held every two years, is considered to be the most prestigious.

Other celebrations revolve around sporting events like football, or surfing championships. Agricultural shows are a popular mix of agricultural excellence and lots of fun with carnival-type entertainments to counter the serious side of produce and livestock judging.

Nationalistic ANZAC Day, which is celebrated across Australia, begins on a more serious note as the bravery of Australia's soldiers at war are remembered in marches and ceremonies, followed by a minute's silence, before everyone adjourns for "a few drinks at the pub" and a chance to reminisce with old mates.

Brisbane's George Street Festival (left) is a carnival of stilt-walkers and Maypole dancers (above), one of the city's happiest times of the year. Agricultural shows (below) are held across the country—a time to display prize bulls or prize pumpkins and a chance for kids to have a great time collecting showbags.

Aboriginal festivals include dances and demonstrations of didgeridoo *music and a chance to revel in cultural roots that have strengthened considerably from a decade or two ago (above right). Christmas, too, is celebrated across the country where people congregate to sing carols and bask in the warmth of community spirit (right). Adelaide's Floral Pageant (below) is another popular festival.*

Moomba

Melbourne's main festival Moomba is celebrated every February during late summer. Deriving from an Aboriginal word, "Moomba" means "Let's get together and have fun" which is exactly what happens. Street amusements and stalls, music, parades, performances and food festivals are all part of the entertainment, culminating in the annual extravaganza of the Moomba Parade.

Sydney's Gay Mardi Gras

Australia's most outrageous festival has to be Sydney's Gay Mardi Gras. A celebration of the unusual, the Mardi Gras gives the opportunity for some of the country's more exotic inhabitants to take to the streets in resplendent displays of outrageousness. Donning wigs, feathers, sequins and plenty of make-up, the celebrants enjoy a parade of highly decorated floats—ending the evening at the all-night Sleaze Ball.

Some of the best known of the Oz Festivals are Melbourne's Moomba where people "get together and have fun" and Sydney's Gay Mardi Gras, where people "get together and have fun" if in a slightly more outrageous manner. Pictures (far left and above top left and right) show the faces of Moomba while those (left and above) show the gorgeous faces of the Mardi Gras.

SYDNEY—OLYMPIC CITY 2000

Australia's premier city Sydney will be the second Australian city to hold the Olympic Games—a grand way to start off the new millennium and a great way to show off the beautiful city to thousands of visitors.

The gleaming glass-and-chrome of the central business district, the renovated Darling Harbour Complex, the Rocks and of course the beaches and the harbour will all be in top form for the new millennium's extravaganza.

One of the reasons Sydney won the bid for the 2000 Olympics was the detail paid to ecological considerations in pre- and post-Olympic preparations—a first and a new consideration for Olympic meetings. The village that will house the more than 10,000 participants and 5,000 team officials is a "solar-powered model for the ecologically sustainable urban life of the future" and the largest solar-powered village in the world.

Already the work done on the 760-hectare Olympic site at Homebush Bay, transforming a disused industrial site back to a natural habitat has won an award for "outstanding achievement for environmental management". The village has more uses in store, after the Games. Directly after the Games it will house participants for the Paraplegic Olympics after which it will provide new private housing.

While Sydney's entry into the Olympic Games requires preparation in the shape of a new stadium (left), this modern city is already primed for international visitors with a sparkling monorail system (top), the spindling remodelled Darling Harbour (right) and of course the stunning Sydney Harbour and Bridge (above).

PART FOUR

ART AND ARCHITECTURE

They say that architecture provides a record of a country's history and it is no less true in Australia. From the stolid colonial buildings of the colony's early days to the later more extravagant buildings that accompanied the gold rush, and the turn-of-the-century Edwardian houses, the styles illustrate the different turns of Australian history and fortunes.

Architecture has not been a conspicuous feature of the Australian landscape. The First Fleet sailed in without any architect at all and the earliest buildings were basic and crude, constructed with whatever materials were at hand. Rough wattle and daub huts with thatched roofs and shuttered windows were the norm. Glass was only to arrive years later.

The classical Georgian style developed to become uniquely Australian, retaining little but the proportional symmetry and harmony of the original, along with the small windows and distinctive doorways. Roofs were extended to produce shading eaves and wide verandahs too, were added—a salient feature of much early Australian architecture. It is a theme repeated from station houses to country pubs and even public buildings.

The Victorian era, fuelled by new wealth from the goldfields, brought radical changes to architecture. Decoration was the key and ebullient displays of wealth created ever more extravagant dwellings for the rich. Speculators made rows and rows of terrace houses, of such style and quality that thousands are still in use today. Decorated with iron lacework, and lovingly restored, they make inner city living an aesthetic pleasure.

With the urban sprawl of the post-war years, a new form of architecture took form. The rather bland triple-fronted brick veneer house, with its own patch of land became the norm, a theme repeated endlessly across the country.

Indigenous styles have yet to fully emerge in Australia, although certain trends are visible. The ecologically sensitive mud brick houses around the artists colony of Eltham outside Melbourne, or the tropical houses of far North Queensland are good examples as are the station houses of the outback which developed with the need to protection from the harsh dry elements. Certain ecologically focused resorts too feature buildings with an eye to harmonious integration with the environment.

Like architecture, the arts have developed slowly. Increased leisure has allowed time for appreciation and a new understanding of the arts—a relatively new situation in a country where creative pursuits were traditionally considered to be unmanly by much of the population. Classical dance, music, opera, theatre and ballet are well established with world-class performers while newer forms of experimental and innovative theatre are still finding their place within the established theatre forms. The most exciting newer area of the arts is the work being done by the Aborigines whose paintings and performances of traditional dance are intriguing audiences around Australia.

Beautifully preserved colonial architecture marks many of Australia's towns and cities like this Victorian era Town Hall in the old gold town of Ballarat (left) and this Anglican Church in Fremantle (above).

A COLONIAL HERITAGE

Australia is a country blessed with an abundance of historical architecture that has survived for over one hundred years. All of the capital cities have well-preserved examples of colonial and 19th century architecture, and in Western Australia, the trading port of Fremantle and the gold town, Kalgoorlie, have marvellous well preserved turn-of-the-century buildings.

The oldest architecture in the country can be found in Hobart and Sydney, cities which both started as stern penal colonies. Their tales are told in the severe cut stone brick buildings, forged by the convicts. Built to last, many are still in use today, over two hundred years later.

Well preserved 19th century residences and government offices are also leftovers from the days as a penal colony. Australians, with their love of conservation, have kept many of the original buildings and while the uses of some have been changed, the outlines remain the same. Walk around Sydney's "Rocks" area and discover an almost perfectly preserved 19th century townscape.

Architecture to gladden the heart and lift the spirits—Sydney's majestic City Hall (left) and the superb Victorian era stained-glass fanlights of the Queen Victoria Building (top left). Renowned for its flamboyant Federation architecture, the gold town of Kalgoorlie has examples galore, such as the Kalgoorlie Hotel (right), or the even more splendid York Hotel (top right). Above: Western Australia's historic town of York is known for its graceful cathedral.

Overleaf: Percy Street in Portland is a perfect example of an Australian rural seaside town. Many older buildings still line the main street.

The Rocks, Sydney

Once the lair of "bawds, seamen and larrikins" Sydney's Rocks area was a wild old place in its prime. Left behind by modern development, it continued almost forgotten right under the southern reaches of the Sydney Harbour Bridge—a backwater missed by the sharp eyes of developers.

Today it is the site of one of Australia's most ambitious redevelopment schemes—as the pristine 19th century townscape has become a prime shopping and lifestyle area with dozens of restaurants to lure the leisurely. Old pubs, shops, and houses have been given a new lease of life with sensitive restoration and renovation while retaining the 19th century flavour. Two of the old hotels, the "Hero of Waterloo" and the "Lord Nelson", have been running continuously since the mid-19th century.

Second only to the Opera House as a tourist attraction, the Rocks is visited by millions of tourists each year.

While the city grows higher and higher with spanking office blocks (right), some of Melbourne's fine old buildings remain, like the landmark Flinder's Street Street Station (top left) and Captain Cook's Cottage (top right). Above: Overlooking the Yarra River is an example of Melbourne's contemporary architecture.

Adelaide is not known as the "City of Churches" for nothing as this fine church (facing page, top left) and the view over the city with its church spires (facing page, bottom) will attest. The Victoria Square Fountain (facing page, top right) adds a modern touch to the surrounding Victorian era architecture.

Melbourne and Adelaide

Established more than a century ago, Melbourne is a treasure house of 19th century architecture as is Adelaide. For a country whose history is so young, anything old or well established is cherished and nothing is more cherished than fine examples of older architecture.

Ebullient and showy facades of Victorian era shops and offices abound in Melbourne's main streets. The riches from the gold rush provided the means for building and the architecture was self-confident and exciting, making it one of the world's best examples of 19th century city architecture. Inner city suburbs are filled with street upon street of fine mid-19th century terraces. Especially large and grand, decorated with acres of iron lace, are the terraces that grace the streets of East Melbourne.

In the city, gracious hundred-year-old shopping arcades like the Block and Royal Arcades are still in use. Unrenovated but well-maintained, the embellished architecture echoes the atmosphere of a more romantic era.

Built as a "Southern Utopia" Adelaide has some of Australia's grandest old homes and a university that echoes the stately lines of England's Oxford. Other grand buildings like the famous Ayer House built in 1846 offer fine examples of sturdy colonial architecture.

AUSTRALIA'S RURAL ARCHITECTURE

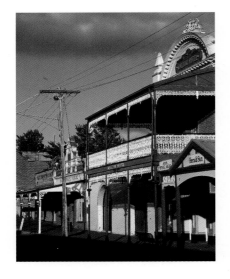

One of the more folksy aspects of Australian architecture is the country pub or hotel where lovely examples are still standing in towns across the country. Many were constructed more than a century ago during the British Victorian era starting in the 1840s when the effects of the Industrial Revolution resulted in mass-produced cast iron. This became a favoured decoration for both rich and poor, with filigreed balustrades, verandahs, pipes and columns all being made or decorated from this material. Even fire grates and staircases were cast from iron.

The hotel's name, often a popular name like the "Station" or "Railway" Hotel, was displayed prominently across the top of the building, an integral part of the decoration. Over the past few years, many of these gorgeous old buildings have been bought up by trendy city dwellers with an eye for style. After sensitive renovations they are run as boutique hotels for discerning city visitors, thus retaining the intrinsic character while changing the menu.

Country pubs tend to play the role of community centres in small towns. Whether small like the famous Ettamogah Pub or the sweetly neat Maldon Hotel (far top left), or larger, like the Cooyar and the purple National Hotels they are instantly recognisable. The interior of the Ettamogah Pub (below left) has a beautiful, typical Australian decor and an ambience that invites relaxation and ... a beer.

The Queensland Tropical House

Seen throughout much of Northern Queensland, the tropical house is a sprawling abode on stilts, based on the same principles as a Malay house. The stilt house is possibly the most typical of all Australian vernacular architecture. Designed for steamy, hot tropical weather, they are built high on stilts of 3 to 3.65 m to allow a cooling air flow above and below the building and also to survive occasional floods. The houses were usually divided by a wide corridor, allowing even more ventilation and verandahs added shade and extra cooling capacity. Examples of this tropical house can be seen dotted throughout Queensland rural areas.

The Australian tropical house (left) allows for a free flow of ventilation both under the house and with a ventilation facility on the rooftop. Another version of the tropical house (above) has less ventilation but more living space, while the "Foot Rot Flats" (top) have little of either.

Overleaf: The Sydney Opera House is one of Australia's most recognisable icons—at least on a par with the Harbour Bridge. The white shells echo the feeling of the sails of the yachts that skim across the harbour every day.

A CONTEMPORARY LANDMARK— THE SYDNEY OPERA HOUSE

Hailed as a contemporary landmark, the Sydney Opera House is Australia's most recognised building—a landmark in more ways than one. This elegant building that captures the grace of sails billowing in the wind makes the perfect counterpoise on the edge of the Harbour.

Started as a project in 1959, it was to attract talk and trouble, controversy and ridicule amongst the conservative sectors for more than a decade. Designed by Danish architect, Jorn Utzon, it stretched not only the imaginations of the people but also the technical and technological limits of the country's engineers of the time.

Spiralling costs, which rose to many more millions than originally estimated, were met with a special lottery to fund it while dissenters predicted disaster. It was finally completed ten years later than estimated, in 1973, at the cost of an unprecedented 102 million dollars (many many times higher than the original 7-million-dollar estimate) and has been a continual source of pride to Sydneysiders ever since. It is Australia's first (and one of the few) buildings of truly international architectural importance.

THE ARTS—MUSIC, DANCE AND DRAMA

Australia's arts scene is growing from strength to strength. While classical music and ballet have been well established for decades, modern theatre and experimental dance are still finding their way, searching for new directions. Aided by generous government grants, and other incentives started in the 70s by the Labour government, the Australian arts scene has received a major shot in the arm.

With the federal government's aim of making the arts accessible to all, up to 2 per cent of the federal government fundings are spent on culture and the arts. Acting as a patron, the government is fostering Australian creativity and the development of new talents, of which the innovative and entertaining Circus Oz is an early example. Operating since the 70s, this circus without animals has toured various countries, delighting new audiences with their clever and amusing antics. Dance and theatre groups are exploring new frontiers, and with this freedom to experiment, strong new directions will emerge.

Australia's music traditions, both classical and modern, have been well established for years, with international recognition of the country's opera singers, classical guitarists and rock music groups. Classical dance and opera too are of high international standards, with luminaries such as Dame Margot Fonteyn, Dame Nellie Melba and Dame Joan Sutherland well known and loved around the world.

Australia's rock groups are legendary. Needing a strong will and a lot of talent to survive in Australia's relatively small but discerning market, a surprising number of musicians have hit the big time internationally. Bands like INXS, Little River Band, the Bee Gees, Men at Work, Savage Garden and ACDC are just a few of those who have found acclaim overseas.

Whether it is classical music (above), jazz (facing page, top left) or opera singing, with famous names like Dame Joan Sutherland (right), Australia holds its own with assurance. Marvellous venues like the Adelaide's Festival Plaza (below) or the ultra-modern Melbourne Arts Centre (facing page, bottom right) make fine showcases for talented performers. These extraterrestrial forms (facing page, bottom left) guard the entrance to Melbourne's National Gallery. Facing page, top right: Homegrown Aussie talents like Paul Hogan have managed to hit the big time internationally.

Some Brilliant Careers
—Australian Film Business

Modern Australian films have been hitting complimentary international headlines over the last twenty years but this was only the end of an industry that started last century. A little known fact is that Australia's movie business started in the very last days of the 19th century with the country's first feature film screened in 1901, an enthusiastic start for a film industry that predated Hollywood. Over 250 silent movies were made in the next 30 years right up until the advent of the "talkies". More films followed but with the success of Hollywood movies, Australia fell into a slump that lasted up till the '70s when the Labour government arts grants provided a major shot in the arm for the ailing industry.

A new wave of films appeared. Taut and tightly directed by a group of young new directors, films like *Picnic At Hanging Rock*, *Caddie* and *Sunday Too Far Away* arrived on the scene to be greeted with critical acclaim both within Australia and internationally.

Since then the list has become endless. *My Brilliant Career*, *Muriel's Wedding*, *Mad Max*, *Strictly Ballroom*, *Crocodile Dundee*, *Gallipoli*, *The Year of Living Dangerously*, and the *Man From Snowy River* are just a few of the successes. Many of the new wave of directors have moved on to Hollywood as have the better actors. While Australia's movie machine is less prolific than Hollywood, India or even France and England, the films are of a quality that make classics.

AUSTRALIAN PAINTERS

Many of Australia's most famous painters were intrigued with the quality of the light and the vivid rawness of the Australian outback. The 19th century painter Tom Roberts was probably one of the first to recognise the wild grandeur. They portrayed the wilderness in stark, graphic terms. Painters like William Dobel, Sidney Nolan, Russell Drysdale, Arthur Boyd, Albert Tucker and more recently, Brett Whitely, found international recognition through their depictions of the wild country—capturing the harshness and imbuing it with the "invisible beauty".

The trend amongst modern painters seems to be an inward movement—leaving the outer world in an attempt to explore the inner realms of consciousness, preferring the abstract to the graphic or figurative. The art scene is thriving with hundreds of small galleries providing opportunity for almost any painter who wants to exhibit.

Sidney Nolan (top right) is one of Australia's most respected painters whose works can be enjoyed at Canberra's Sidney Nolan Gallery (right). Paintings play a part in Aussie life. Even some pubs (left) feature paintings along with the beer. Outside murals (above), like this one in Alice Springs, is a popular art form.

Aboriginal Art—A Distinctive Tradition

When painter Pablo Picasso was shown paintings made by the Gunwingu people, an Arnhem Land tribe, he is said to have remarked "This is what I've been trying to achieve all my life." The purity of line, the integrity of shape and form is what Aboriginal portrayals are all about.

Since the 1970s the recognition of Aboriginal art has grown to become somewhat of a trend. Traditionally, Aboriginal art stems from religious beliefs and that used for decoration. They used a mix of four basic colours derived from the earth—red, black, white, and yellow or ochre, colours taken from the natural substances of ochres, clays, manganese, charcoal, orchid juices, eggs and blood. Brushes were made of human hair or frayed bark and chewed sticks. Sometimes they used their hands either as a utensil, or as a stencil to paint around.

The human body was the main canvas. Caves, wood bark and memorial posts were also used to portray the simple geometric and stylised shapes. Symbolism is a key element. Animals and spirit figures from the Dreamtime are portrayed in beautiful pure forms—recognisable but not realistic. In sites scattered across the Northern Territory, in Arnhem Land, Pilbarra, Kakadu and the Cape York Peninsula, are numerous examples of prehistoric rock art at its most elaborate, some of which dates back 40,000 years.

While earlier painters like the talented Albert Namatjira made landscape watercolours in a Western style, the newer waves of painters are drawing from their roots to produce exciting works, following traditional styles. Sand drawings and body paintings are being translated onto canvas, to be snapped up by an ever more appreciative international public.

A growing recognition of the unique visions of Aboriginal art has led to a resurgence as well as exciting new horizons and a growing demand. Ian Abdullah of Alice Springs (top) is applying old techniques to modern paintings while Jilly Stockman (above) is expanding the boundaries of traditional design. Bark paintings too have gained a new popularity (right), while a group of women paint up a storm (far right).

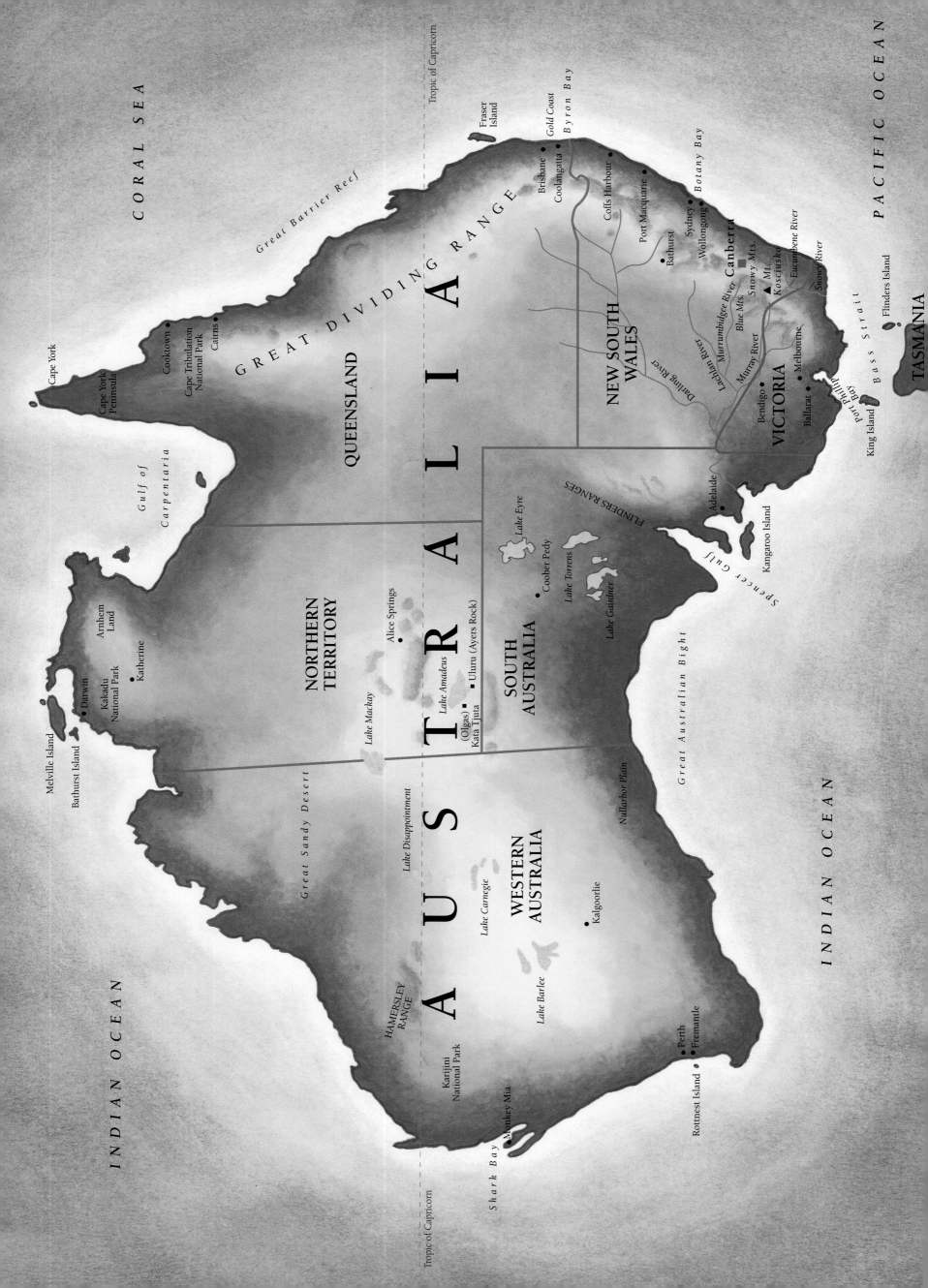